DESERT STORM
THE GULF WAR IN COLOUR

SERGIO ROMANO

Greenhill Books

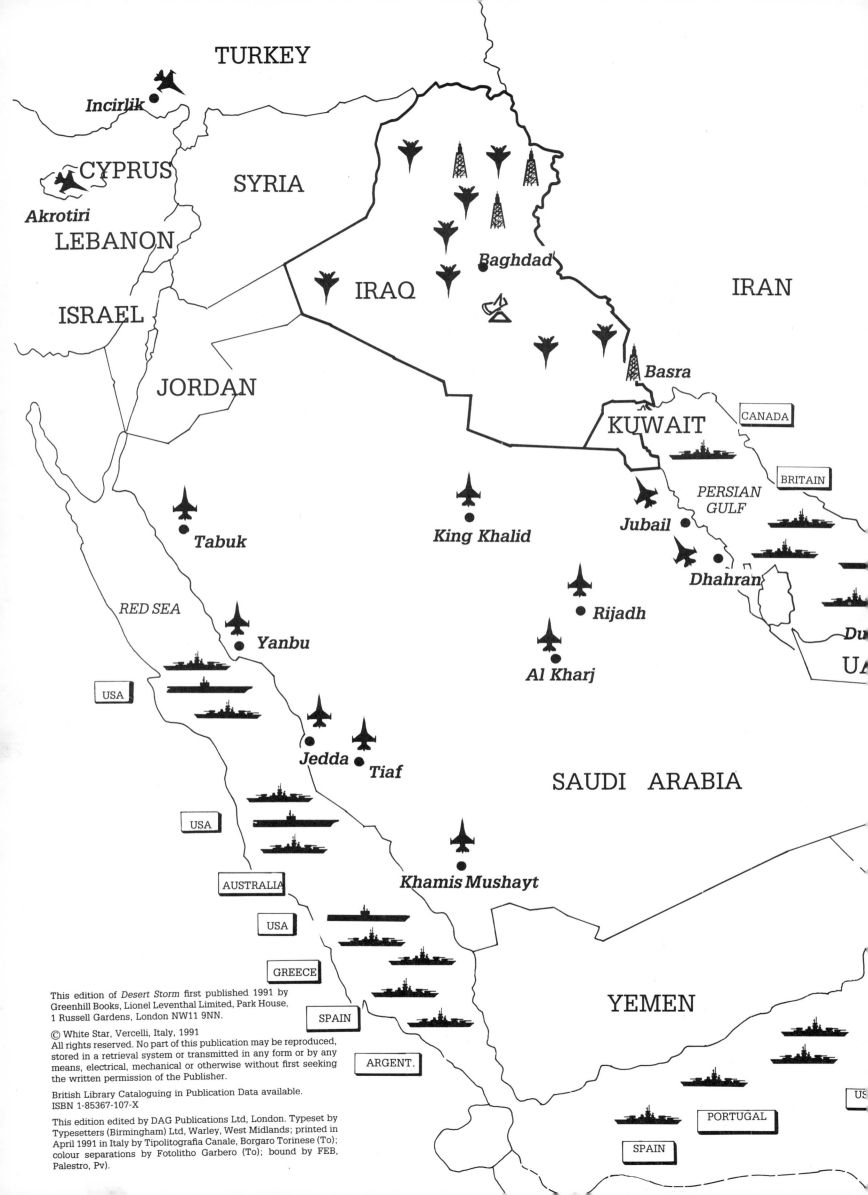

TURKEY

Incirlik

CYPRUS

SYRIA

Akrotiri

LEBANON

ISRAEL

IRAQ

Baghdad

IRAN

JORDAN

Basra

KUWAIT

CANADA

PERSIAN
GULF

BRITAIN

Tabuk

King Khalid

Jubail

Dhahran

RED SEA

Yanbu

Rijadh

USA

Al Kharj

Du

UA

USA

Jedda *Tiaf*

SAUDI ARABIA

USA

AUSTRALIA

USA

Khamis Mushayt

GREECE

This edition of *Desert Storm* first published 1991 by
Greenhill Books, Lionel Leventhal Limited, Park House,
1 Russell Gardens, London NW11 9NN.

© White Star, Vercelli, Italy, 1991

British Library Cataloguing in Publication Data available.
ISBN 1-85367-107-X

This edition edited by DAG Publications Ltd, London. Typeset by
Typesetters (Birmingham) Ltd, Warley, West Midlands; printed in
April 1991 in Italy by Tipolitografia Canale, Borgaro Torinese (To);
colour separations by Fotolitho Garbero (To); bound by FEB,
Palestro, Pv).

SPAIN

YEMEN

ARGENT.

PORTUGAL

SPAIN

US

Text
by Sergio Romano

Editorial coordination
by Valeria Manferto de Fabianis

Design
by Patrizia Balocco Lovisetti

Editorial consultant
Fabio Bourbon

THE ANTI-IRAQ COALITION, Countries and Contributions

USA: More than 400,000 men including 200,000 army troops, and 90,000 Marines with more than 1,000 tanks and 2,000 other armoured vehicles; 40,000 airmen with 1,300 combat aircraft and 1,500 helicopters; 30,000 sailors aboard 80 ships including 6 aircraft carriers. The American contingent included 30,000 women.

Saudi-Arabia: More than 100,000 men including those of the National Guard, with 550 tanks, 16,500 airmen with 180 aircraft, 7,200 sailors aboard 8 frigates.

Argentina: 900 men on board 2 ships.

Australia: 600 men on board 3 ships, 2 medical units.

Bahrain: 2,300 men, 4,500 airmen, 600 sailors.

Bangladesh: More than 2,500 men.

Belgium: Contribution of men and matériel under the aegis of NATO's ACE rapid intervention force.

Canada: 1,700 sailors aboard 3 ships, a squadron of F-18 combat aircraft.

Czechoslovakia: 170 men in a military unit specializing in chemical warfare.

South Korea: A transport aircraft and a team of doctors.

Denmark: A corvette in the Gulf and some Sidewinder missiles sent to Turkey.

Egypt: 19,000 men with the support of ground-to-air missiles.

United Arab Emirates: 40,000 men with 200 armoured vehicles; 1,500 airmen with 80 combat aircraft; 1,500 sailors aboard 15 ships.

France: 18,000 men with 160 tanks, 24 aircraft, 120 helicopters, 11 ships.

Germany: Contribution of men and matériel under the aegis of NATO's ACE force.

Great Britain: 28,000 men with 160 tanks, 102 armoured vehicles and 108 combat vehicles; 4,000 airmen with 6 squadrons of strike aircraft; 72 aircraft, 40 helicopters and 3 maritime reconnaissance aircraft; 3,000 sailors aboard 20 ships.

Greece: 200 men and 1 ship.

Italy: 1,335 sailors aboard 5 ships; 10 aircraft with 600 pilots and airmen, as well as a contribution under the aegis of NATO's ACE.

Kuwait: About 22,000 men of whom 15,000 were regular soldiers and 7,000 volunteers.

Morocco: 5,000 men with some light vehicles.

New Zealand: 2 transport aircraft and a military medical team.

Niger: 500 men.

Norway: A support ship.

Netherlands: 400 sailors aboard 2 ships.

Oman: 25,000 men with some tanks, 63 combat aircraft and 4 attack craft with Exocet missiles.

Pakistan: 10,000 men.

Poland: 2 ships, a field hospital, and a medical team.

Qatar: Unspecified number of men and aircraft.

Senegal: 500 men.

Syria: About 21,000 men with 300 armoured vehicles.

Spain: 500 men and 3 ships.

Hungary: a medical team.

BELG.

NETHS.

GULF OF OMAN

●Muscat

Masirah

MAN

ITALY

USA

AY

INDIAN OCEAN

N

IRAQI FORCES in the Kuwait Theatre of Operations

900,000 men including 6 divisions of the Republican Guard, 700 aircraft, 300 helicopters, 4,200 tanks, 70 ships, 3,000 artillery pieces.

THE GULF:
From the Crisis to the War

When Iraqi troops invaded Kuwait at dawn on 2 August 1990, the eyes of the West had been fixed for some time on events in the USSR and eastern Europe. We were aware that Saddam Hussein had sent threatening signals to the government of Emir Al Sabah, but perhaps one could be forgiven for thinking that this was yet another bout of sabre-rattling in the seemingly endless volatility of the Middle East. Yet the Gulf crisis that was about to hold the world in thrall had both remote and recent origins. Let us try to reconstruct them, beginning with the aggressor.

Iraq is not a state with a long history; it has no natural frontiers and is not inhabited by an Iraqi nation with a strong character and a cultural and religious homogeneity. Of its population of about 17,000,000, Arabs make up 72 per cent, Kurds 22 per cent, and Turkomans and other ethnic groups 6 per cent. Ninety seven per cent of the population are Muslims, but they are divided into Shi'ites (51 per cent) and Sunnis (46 per cent), that is to say the two large rival sects into which Islam divided after the death of the Prophet. Iraq's birth as a state dates back to the First World War. In a bid to defeat the Turks, who were allied with Imperial Germany, the British held out the prospect of the creation of a large Arab kingdom stretching from the Persian Gulf to the Mediterranean, to Hussein of Hejaz, a Hashemite prince from the Arabian peninsula. But, in May 1916, with the secret Sykes-Picot Pact, the British and French agreed on the division of the Arab provinces of the Ottoman Empire with France gaining Syria and Lebanon, and Britain Mesopotamia and Palestine. When, in 1919, Hussein's son Feisal, who was the fraternal companion of Lawrence of Arabia in the anti-Turkish guerrilla war of the preceding years, took possession of Damascus, and had himself proclaimed king, the French landed in Syria and demanded their share.

So as not completely to discontent their Hashemite allies, the British redrew the map of the Middle East at Whitehall with a few pen strokes. This created the Kingdom of Iraq for Feisal by uniting the Ottoman provinces of Baghdad, Basra and Mosul into a single country. To Feisal's brother, Abdullah, Britain gave an emirate, by separating the territories to the east of the River Jordan from Palestine, keeping for herself a Mandate over Palestine from the River Jordan to the sea and, naturally, keeping a protectorate over the vassal states that she had created for the two brothers of the Hashemite dynasty. To separate Iraq from Iran, Britain chose the historic border between the Ottoman and Persian Empires; the border with Turkey was an administrative one, which had separated the *vilayet* of Mosul from the other Ottoman provinces, while the borders with Syria, Arabia and Kuwait were simply drawn with a ruler. These borders were fixed between a cup of tea and a glass of whisky, and Winston Churchill commented that they smacked more of the latter than of the former.

These borders were of very minor importance because Great Britain frequently exercised guardianship on both sides of the frontier, albeit wearing two different hats. Britain's protectorate over Kuwait, for example, dated from 1899 and, together with a strong interest in the exploitation of the oil riches in the region, enabled her to keep an eye on the Gulf, the route to the Indies and the southern 'glacis' of Russian power.

Of all the artificial creations thought out by Great Britain to guarantee control over a large number of the provinces of the former Ottoman Empire, Iraq soon showed itself to be the most unruly and unpredictable. To govern this state, King Feisal made use of the Sunni minority. He died in 1933, a year after the end of the British Protectorate, and admission to the League of Nations as an independent state. He was succeeded by his son, Ghazi, and, after the latter's death in an accident, by Ghazi's son, Feisal II, who was flanked by a regency council.

Then, in 1936, after some ethnic clashes in the north of the country, Iraq had its first military proconsul in the person of a general named Bakr Sidqi, who had become a national hero after brutally repressing the revolt of a Christian minority, the Assyrians. Welcomed by triumphal arches, decorated with ghoulish symbols – melons stained with blood and pierced by dagger blades – Bakr Sidqi forced the King to accept the 'change of the guard' in which he himself kept the position of commander of the armed forces. In this way a new politico-military caste appeared among the leaders of the state and its ideology – if one can call it such – was nationalistic. It was also anti-British and anti-progressive, and had strong sympathies for, and affinities with, the totalitarian and authoritarian regimes that had come to power in numerous European countries during the preceding years. I said 'nationalistic', but in a country without history, and national traditions, the nationality of the new military classes had no arguments to nurture it except the pretentious representation of a non-existent past, the invention of an enemy and the recurring crusades in pursuit of a national aim. These are the very ingredients that we will find many years later in Saddam Hussein's policies.

After the outbreak of the Second World War, the most overtly pro-Fascist of the authoritarian faction of the Iraqi ruling class seized power and called on the Axis powers to aid them. But the British occupied Basra, and Germany hesitated before becoming deeply involved in an adventure that would have distracted her from the Russian and European theatres of operations, while Italy limited herself to sending a few aircraft. Within a few weeks, the British marched on Baghdad and took control of the country once more. From then until 1958, Iraq remained in the British sphere of influence, and became a 'fifth column' of pro-Western Arabism in a world in which anti-imperialist and anti-Zionist slogans were becoming ever more insistently the legitimate ideology of the new ruling classes.

While Nasser seized power in Egypt, Iraq, thanks to Nuri-al-Said, an old prime minister of proven British loyalties, formed a political and military alliance with Iran and Turkey – the 1954 Baghdad Pact. This was an extension of the anti-Soviet line-up of NATO into the near East and it did not hesitate to support the Anglo-French expedition into Suez two years later. But in 1958 Iraq precipitated herself once more into the spiral of civil conflict, as had happened in 1936 when the military, led by General Kassim, staged a *coup d'état*. But now, instead of limiting themselves to taking power and leaving the existing institutional forms intact, they brutally murdered the King, the royal family and Nuri-al-Said, proclaimed a Republic and denounced the Baghdad Pact. In those years of Cold War, the Iraqi revolution was immediately interpreted in Washington as the first signal of a phenomenon that risked spreading to other countries in the region and threatening the East-West equilibrium.

In the following days, an American expeditionary force of 10,000 men landed at Beirut and 2,500 British paratroops established themselves in Amman. Paradoxically the Americans, with a debatable sense of timing, were now doing exactly what they had prevented the British and French doing two years previously, in much more resolute circumstances. The crisis did not last long because the worries of the United States turned out to be exaggerated but 14 July 1958 marked a turning-point none the less. From that day on, Iraq ceased to be an ally of the West in the Arab world and set out to become, with the inevitable adjustments

and haggling of Middle East politics, a travelling companion of Soviet policy in that region. This anti-Western evolution was emphasized when power passed from the hands of the military into those of a national and socialist party known as Baath, whose foundation was largely due to the efforts of a Christian intellectual, Michel Aflak, a Syrian of partially French origin.

With the Baath Party, whose name means rebirth and revival, secular Arabism finally had a social national ideology to which those classes and tribal groupings who aspired to assume the leadership of the country could have recourse in order to legitimize themselves. However, in the Baath Party, or to be more precise, in the use which Arab politicians have made of its ideology, there is a potential contradiction. The ideology postulates the revival and the unity of the Arab nation, but its exponents have generally exploited the mobilizing power of this idea to strengthen their own state and their control over their national society. This has led to a continuous equivocal oscillation between Arabism as the banner of all Arabs and Arabism as a pretext for the hegemonic ambitions of rival states such as Iraq and Syria, who both claimed to be inspired by the self-same Baathist ideology. The Palestinians have often been the victims of this misunderstanding.

Now a new man appears in the sphere of the Iraqi Baath. His name is Saddam Hussein, and he was born in 1937 near Takrit, on the River Tigris, in Sunni territory, 170 kilometres north of Baghdad. Family legend has it that he spent his formative years in the home of an uncle, Khayrallah Tulfah, who had participated in the pro-Fascist *coup* in 1941, and from that experience had acquired a deep hatred for British imperialism, Nourished by the memories of his uncle, Saddam became a member of Baath at the age of 21, took part in an abortive attempt on the life of Kassim, and fled to Syria and Egypt before returning to Baghdad in 1963, immediately after a group of Baathists and Arab nationalist officers had overthrown the regime and killed its leader. He was only 26 years old, but the essential characteristics of his personality were already evident. He was violent, unruly, stubborn and cruel. It was he who interrogated and tortured the political prisoners in the palace in which King Feisal and his family had been brutally assassinated. However, his efficiency and organizational qualities made a favourable impression on Michel Aflak, who paved the way for him to take up a post in the Baath regional command, a sort of politbureau that decided the political strategy of the party. This was the start of the irresistible rise of Saddam Hussein. In 1966, while the Baath was once more in opposition he founded the secret police, and in 1968 as soon as Baath regained power, he became Number Two in the regime under the presidency of Ahmed Hassan al-Bakr.

In 1979 he took the place of al-Bakr and established himself as leader of the country. All the rest – the attack on Iran, the use of chemical weapons, the massacre of the Kurds, the enormously large arms purchases on all world markets, the destruction of an Iraqi nuclear reactor by the Israeli Air Force, the attempted construction of a super-cannon for launching nuclear warheads, the hanging of a British journalist guilty only of excessive professional curiosity, the financial and territorial dispute with Kuwait, the invasion of the Emirate – is recent news.

It is worthwhile trying to discover the broad lines of the policy behind this sequence of events. In other words, what are the intentions and the aims for which Saddam Hussein dragged his country into a war that lasted eight years. Without doubt, Iran's Islamic revolution represented a threat to the Baghdad regime. As well as being fundamentally different, the Iran of the Ayatollahs is Shi'ite, fundamentalist and theocratic, while Saddam's Iraq is Sunni, secular and modernizing. The two countries have more long-standing reasons for conflict and above all they both have the means to render life reciprocally impossible.

Iran had a Shi'ite Fifth Column within the Iraqi regime, and Iraq in its turn could incite the Arab and Kurdish minorities against the Persian and Shi'ite hegemony of the Ayatollah. The war broke out in September 1980 when Saddam attacked Iran without warning. This he did after having informed the Soviets of his plan, and in the conviction that he could rapidly exploit the weakness, instability and isolation of the Iranian regime. And he probably also did it in the belief that nothing would have exalted the function of his regime and create an Iraqi nation as much as a rapid military triumph. But the war lasted eight years, and it was the most atrocious and bloody ever to have been fought in the region. Saddam won in the end, if it is possible to speak of victory in such circumstances, because as the war went on he had the tacit alliance of all those countries – the United States, the Soviet Union, the Gulf states and some western European states – who were greatly alarmed by Khomeini's revolution.

Funded by the Arab states, armed by the Soviets and some of the major armaments industries of the West, Saddam thus became the head of the most powerful and highly indebted state in the region.

It has been calculated that he imported weapons to the value of $42.8 billion dollars between 1982 and 1989, and that in those years he constantly spent on armaments a sum equal to 50 per cent of the GNP. It has also been calculated that in the last five years Iraq's purchases of arms represented nine per cent of the total world arms sales. According to Judith Miller and Laurie Mylroie, authors of an excellent book published at the beginning of the crisis (*Saddam Hussein and the Crisis in the Gulf*, Times Books and Random House), Iraq's main suppliers were the Soviet Union (40 per cent), China (13 per cent) and the countries of western Europe (15 per cent), of which France had the lion's share. Iraq paid for these massive arms purchases with its oil revenue and loans from other Arab countries and from Kuwait in particular.

The long war had another consequence, that of making Saddam's regime increasingly more oppressive, cruel and ambitious, and turning the country into a police state. While sacrificing his subjects in bloody battles, he carried out continuous 'purges' in the political and administrative structures of the state. Saddam also created a fictitious imperial past for Iraq, proclaiming himself a descendant of Nabucco, claiming the legal heritage of great Hammurabi and surrounding himself with an increasing number of officials who staged the cult of his personality in increasingly magniloquent rites.

When the war ended, with a million dead, and an apparent victory, he immediately set about preparing for new exploits. To wipe out the debts and gain new sources of revenue to translate into reality the power that he believed himself to have acquired with his victory over Iran, as well as to ensure better access to the sea and to assert his political and military hegemony in the Gulf region, Saddam turned on Kuwait in the summer of 1990.

It was not the first time that Iraq had attempted to take possession of the Emirate. Kassim had tried in June 1961, but the British had sent a small task force to the Gulf and made it clear to the Iraqi dictator that they would not tolerate the annexation. Some Arab and Muslim states – Saudi Arabia, Egypt and Iran – had supported the Emirate, and Kassim was forced to give up his plan. To try once more, Saddam needed an excuse. He put some contentious issues on the table: payment of the loans granted during the war, exploitation of the oil wells on the border and oil price policies. But he abandoned them as soon as he thought the moment for action had come.

Like Kassim, he too claimed that historically Kuwait was a province of Iraq. This was an allusion to the fact that the Ottoman Empire in an attempt to affirm its sovereignty over the Emirate, had formally annexed it to Basra, one of the three provinces with which the British had formed the state of Iraq after the First World War. But he neglected to recall that the Turks had always exercised only nominal control over Kuwait and that Iraq itself was a recent political creation. As in the crisis with Iran eleven years before, he chose his moment after examining the international situation. He knew the events of 1989 had weakened the USSR and that, unlike in the past, Iraq would not be able to count on the support of a world power. But, at the same time, he was convinced that the end of the Cold War gave him greater room to manoeuvre. If he had tried to annex Kuwait some years previously, he would have aroused the opposition of the United States, which would never have permitted a Soviet ally to become the dominant power in the Gulf. Indeed, the Soviet Union itself would have held Saddam back to avoid being involved in a world war to satisfy the ambitions of a vassal. Now in completely different circumstances – at least Saddam probably reasoned so – the operation was finally possible. The conversation that he had with the US Abassador at the end of July, the transcription of which we read last September, must have convinced him that the Americans would have accepted a fait accompli. At dawn on 2 August, Iraqi tanks crossed the border and rapidly took possession of the Emirate.

However, Saddam was not the only one to interpret the events of 1989 as opening new perspectives. For President Bush's America, the end of the Cold War offered the prerequisites for a new world order in which the United States would be the major actor. The dream of Wilson and Roosevelt was finally within reach after forty years, in the course of which the United States had continuously found its path blocked by the hegemonic plans and ambitions of an enemy power. While Saddam saw 1989 as giving him the chance to modify the equilibrium of the region to his own advantage, Bush saw 1989 as giving him the chance of finally realizing the grand international design that

America had pursued in alternate phases ever since its entry into the First World War.

While Saddam thought the moment had finally arrived to realize an old Iraqi ambition, Bush considered the occupation of Kuwait as an intolerable challenge to the new world order he wanted to construct. In this clash between two different interpretations, there are the germs of the war that was to break out five months later. Bolstered by his extraordinary diplomatic and political experience – he had represented his country in Peking and at the United Nations, and had been director of the CIA and Vice President of the USA – Bush soon showed himself to be a capable manager of the crisis. International circumstances were in his favour. The smaller nations could not endorse an act of violence that risked providing a useful precedent for any other country wanting to satisfy its territorial ambitions at the expense of its neighbour.

The majority of Arab countries could not tolerate the idea that one of their number was turning into the Prussia of the Middle East. The Europeans could not accept a gesture that would expose them to the risk of being subjected to perpetual blackmail by a single nation. And finally the Soviet Union was too interested in its new relationship with the United States to sacrifice it to the advantage of an adventurer who had not even informed them of his intentions.

The Saudi Arabian invitation to station troops on its soil and this extraordinary convergence of interests led President Bush to send the first contingent of American forces to the Gulf, and to organize a vast anti-Iraqi coalition within a few days. For its part, the United Nations supplied the necessary legal endorsement and de facto authorized America to act in the name of the international community.

One will understand the history of the last few months better when one is able to view the events with a greater detachment and can consult the documentation, which has to a great extent remained secret. But the management of the crisis by its main protagonists might suggest some considerations one can make here and now.

Let us begin with Saddam. Everything points to the fact that his strategy – from the invasion of Kuwait to the final negotiations of Tariq Aziz in Moscow during that brief period of negotiations that preceded land operations – was completely dominated by his precise convictions about the vulnerability of the West and the USA in particular. He began by thinking that the presence of several thousand foreign hostages would force the West to adopt a more conciliatory and permissive attitude. When he realized that this attempt at blackmail only increased world indignation and did not intimidate governments, he was forced to free them. He continued to believe, up to the last moment, that Western opinion and American public opinion in particular, would not tolerate the sight of their own dead on television. Then he probably thought that the pacifist movement would have submerged Western societies like a river in flood and would paralyse government action. He committed another error by thinking that Israel would be unable to resist his provocations and would take up arms. He also believed that the entry of Israel into the war would sow discord in the field of his Arab enemies and destroy the unity of the anti-Iraq coalition. He did not foresee that the Americans would manage to persuade Israel to practise moderation and above all that the launching of Scud missiles on Israeli cities would provoke waves of disapproval and anger − and not only in the West. He did manage, it is true, to gain the sympathy of the Palestinians and Arab masses in Jordan, Algeria and Morocco, but he greatly overestimated the importance of Arab and Islamic feeling in a conflict that involved the concrete interests of some of the major countries in the region.

The contrasting images of the days immediately following the truce − the frustration of the Palestinians in Amman and the Occupied Territories, the joy of the liberated population of Kuwait − demonstrate just to what extent the unity of the Arab world is still ephemeral and precarious. Naturally, he made other mistakes, including that of undervaluing the technology of the American war machine and of thinking that it would not play a decisive role in the struggle. His greatest error was that of believing in an image of the USA and the West that had no connection with reality. There was perhaps only one excusing factor: his view regarding the West, and its probable reaction was after all the same view that emerged from a large section of the Western media. It was the newspapers, radio and television of the 'enemy' that continued to stress the vulnerability of public opinion, the wavering of governments, the importance of pacifist movements and the strategic unpredictability of war in the desert, which would be a hard test for refined war technology. We can conclude by saying that the United States and the West in general defeated Saddam twice. Once with the extraordinary firepower of one of the major military expeditions in history, and once with successive waves of involuntary disinformation. While Saddam Hussein trapped himself in the vicious circle of his erroneous perceptions about the state of the moral health of the adversary, and increasingly limited his own margin for manoeuvre, President Bush showed a great spirit of steadfastness and extraordinary imperturbability.

This does not mean that he was devoid of uncertainties or that he followed the same strategic line right from the beginning. A radical change of course took place after the American elections in November. Until a few days beforehand, the President of the United States had officially put his faith in the efficacy of the embargo. From then on he resolutely chose the way of the ultimatum and of the military threat. We can only make guesses about the reasons for such a change. For example, we may suppose that he had planned it for some time, but wanted to avoid the interference and the tiresome buzzing of the electoral campaign that would have adverse influence on the military intervention. We could also suppose that after a few weeks of embargo and the realistic evaluation of its effects, he reached negative conclusions. In Bush's eye the embargo probably presented some disadvantages. It would only have been effective if applied with firmness for a very long time, but to this end it would have been necessary firmly to hold the reins of the anti-Iraq coalition and prepare American public opinion for a long wait. This was probably the factor that persuaded Bush to change strategy so abruptly. If Saddam wrongly thought that American public opinion would not have tolerated the impact of a war and the sight of blood, Bush, much more realistically, knew that it would prefer a decisive show of strength to a long tiresome siege. There was still, it must be said, a risk − that America, as predicted by Saddam, would rapidly succumb to the syndrome of Vietnam. But as soon as the military operations had begun, it was clear that the President of the United States and the American armed forces had thoroughly learned the lessons of Vietnam and would not fight as they had twenty years previously in front of the TV cameras.

In spite of the enormous deployment of the world's media, the Gulf War is one of the least observed and described wars in history. American bombing 'softened up' the Iraqi forces and convinced Saddam that he had no hope of winning the war. It was the American domination of the skies that led a large part of the Iraqi air force to seek refuge in Iran. It was the electronic tracking systems that, right from the first days, probably threw into confusion the command and control systems of the Iraqi forces. It was the Patriot missile that to a great extent neutralized the Scuds and strongly reduced the blackmail of terror that Saddam Hussein had hoped to exercise on the populations of Israel and the Gulf States. However, up to the final days of the conflict, he still had the possibility of saving, if not the whole of Kuwait, at least a part of the 19th Province and the bulk of his military forces. In this phase the Soviet Union was of great help to him. There, after the resignation of Eduard Shevardnadze, and the prevalence of the conservative faction, an authoritarian solution seemed to be in the pipeline. During the previous months, the Soviets had sacrificed Saddam to the new relationship they intended to establish with the United States, and they had taken the side of the anti-Iraq coalition, although without getting involved militarily. This decision had provoked the anger of the conservatives as well as a considerable section of the armed forces, who were convinced that in this course the Soviet Union was abdicating its position of power in the Middle East. It was for this reason that, after the resignation of Shevardnadze, Gorbachev undertook diplomatic efforts to impose a negotiated settlement on the Americans. Had he succeeded in his intentions, Moscow would have reaffirmed the importance of its role in the region, strengthened its links with Iraq and saved the armed forces of a client state, the main part of whose arsenal had been supplied by the 'military and industrial complex' of the Soviet Union.

In other words, with its diplomacy the USSR hoped to reconquer, along with a more general influence in the Middle East, an ally and a client. The attempt failed for a number of reasons: the steadfastness of the Americans, the Soviet desire not to push its mediation too far and prejudice its relationship with the United States and, above all, the attitude of Saddam who must have hoped up to the last minute to turn to his own ends the desire for peace expressed by public opinion in the West and thus refused to accept immediately those conditions that would have halted the American forces on the borders of a liberated Kuwait. Perhaps he was a victim of his own shrewdness. Perhaps he did not understand that there is always a moment in international relations when astuteness, if pushed to its most extreme consequence, becomes a suicide weapon. We do not yet know what the medium term results of the Gulf War will be; however we do know that even though its land operations lasted only one hundred hours and were confined to a small area of the Middle East between the Persian Gulf and Mesopotamia, this was not a 'regional' war. Unlike the wars that have been fought in the region during the course of the last forty-three years, from the Arab-Israeli conflict of 1948 to the war between Iran and Iraq in the 1980s, it has not only modified the political and military equilibrium of the Middle East but has affected world equilibrium. In fact, like all great wars, the Gulf War also annunciates in a brutal manner some truths that none will be able to ignore in the years to come. We know that the United States can put half a million men in the field almost 10,000 kilometres away from their home territory and deploy a military technology that in a few days revolutionized the 'art of war'.

We know that the USSR, for all her strength on a military level, is no longer capable of opposing American actions in an area that is so close to its natural interests. We know that the United Nations can take note of international consensus and play a useful part in such a perspective, but that it is incapable of imposing its will on an aggressor unless a great power takes responsibility for the action. We know that Iraqi military power has ceased to represent a threat for the other states in the region. We know that Europe, despite the considerable efforts it has made on its way to unity, is completely unsuited to facing up to a military crisis and is destined to reveal its traditional and national divisions in such a situation.

Finally, we know that Arab unity is an important emotional factor for the political conscience of the region; it can express frustration, resentment and aspiration, but it cannot yet transform itself into political power and influence events in the Middle East. And we also know that the American victory, while ending an intolerable episode of international violence, does not solve the great problems of the region: the Arab-Israeli conflict, the creation of a Palestinian state, economic progress, modernization and secularization of Arab countries. These are the facts from which it will be necessary to set out in the months to come if we wish to avoid a situation where the Gulf conflict remains but one episode in a long saga of warfare destined to disturb the political and economic equilibrium of the Middle East for years to come.

Chronology of Events

2 August Iraqi troops enter Kuwait and occupy Kuwait City; the Emir takes refuge in Saudi Arabia.

4 August The EEC and Japan impose a total embargo on petroleum products from Iraq and Kuwait.

6 August The United Nations vote for economic and military sanctions against Iraq.

7 August Saudi Arabia declares that it is willing to allow American troops and aircraft to enter its territory. The American aircraft carriers, *Independence* and *Saratoga*, the battleship *Wisconsin* and the helicopter ship *Inchon*, with a battalion of Marines, sail for the Persian Gulf. The aircraft carrier *Eisenhower* moves from the eastern Mediterranean towards the Arabian Sea, passing through the Suez Canal with Egypt's permission.

8 August Operation 'Desert Shield' begins: American F-15s and paratroops enter Saudi Arabia, while Italy, Spain and Germany guarantee logistic support to the US forces.

9 August Turkey allows the number of American soldiers on its territory to be increased. Great Britain and France decide to aid the United States by sending aircraft and ground forces to the Gulf. Syria and Iran announce that they are considering sending troops, while the USSR declares that it does not exclude sending a contingent to form part of a UN military force.

11 August Soldiers from Egypt and Morocco disembark in Saudi Arabia.

12 August President Bush orders a blockade to be conducted discreetly so as not to appear an act of open warfare.

15 August The aircraft carrier *Kennedy* heads for the Mediterranean.

16 August Saddam Hussein tells the world that, in the event of war, a large number of Americans will go back home 'in body bags'.

18 August Iraq formalizes its intention of using the Westerners present in the country as hostages.

20 August Iraq's insistence that the Gulf crisis is linked to the solution of the Palestinian problem does not meet with credibility in the West.

22 August American military presence in Saudi Arabia continues to be reinforced.

25 August The United Nations approves the use of 'minimal force' to ensure that the embargo is respected.

28 August Armoured divisions and troop transport vehicles arrive in Saudi Arabia.

6 September There are now 100,000 soldiers lined up in the Gulf region.

10 September The United States asks the European nations to send troops to support the UN initiative.

28 September The United Nations Security Council denounces Iraq's attempt to link the Gulf crisis with the Palestinian problem; separate solutions must be found.

30 September The USSR refuses to send a contingent of troops to the Gulf to support the Allies, while the French send more troops to reinforce their own presence.

2 October After almost two months of sailing, the aircraft carrier *Independence* enters the Persian Gulf.

14 October Iraq subordinates its withdrawal from Kuwait to the right to maintain possession of the small islands of Wamba and Bubiyan.

15 October For the first time, President Bush hints at the possibility of putting the responsible Iraqis on trial for war crimes at the end of the war.

16 October The first organized pacifist demonstration takes place in the United States. The movement, though widespread, does not manage to find much support among the vast majority of Americans, who support Bush's actions.

19 October The American President abruptly reaffirms that negotiations will only take place after a complete and unconditional Iraqi withdrawal from Kuwait.

30 October American Marines begin manoeuvres in Oman.

4 November James Baker, the American Secretary of State, visits the troops in Saudi Arabia.

5 November At a meeting between King Fahd and Baker, the command structures for the forces in Saudi Arabia are worked out.

8 November 140,000 troops arrive to join the forces already deployed in the Gulf region. This time they come with the declared intention of providing support for a possible military offensive.

13 November The battleship *Missouri* sails for the Gulf.

15 November Allied military manoeuvres on the Kuwaiti border increase in intensity.

18 November Iraq announces the liberation of Western hostages within two months.

19 November Saddam Hussein announces his intention to send large numbers of troops to Kuwait in response to the reinforcement of Allied forces.

20 November On America's Thanksgiving Day, President Bush visits the troops in Saudi Arabia. The UN approves military action after the ultimatum expires.

15 January Midnight New York time: the UN ultimatum to Iraq expires.

16 January, morning Iraq declares that it has won the war because the ultimatum has expired without any reaction on the part of the Allies.

16 January, night The Allied offensive begins. The air forces drop thousands of tons of explosives on Iraq in three hours.

18 January Eight Scud missiles are launched by Iraq against Israel. An Italian Tornado is reported missing on its first mission.

19 January Further missile attacks on Israel induce America to send military advisers and batteries of Patriot anti-missile missiles to Jerusalem.

21 January Iraq announces that the captured pilots who had been shown on TV several days before, in an infamous attempt at propaganda, will be used as human shields to defend military targets.

25 January The destruction of Kuwaiti oil terminals by Iraq marks the start of an ecological catastrophe, with millions of barrels of crude oil flowing into the sea.

26 January The first Iraqi aircraft take refuge in Iran. Before the end of the war, more than 100 aircraft will have sought safety at Iranian airfields where they run no risk of being pounded by Allied bombers.

30 January Iraqi troops engage Allied defences around the city of Khafji. The attack is repulsed after 38 hours of fighting.

13 February A Smart bomb, launched by a Stealth bomber, hits an air-raid shelter in Baghdad, causing numerous deaths.

15 February Baghdad begins diplomatic manoeuvres to get out of a war that appears to be already lost, but the first attempts are clumsy and unconvincing. The proposed withdrawal from Kuwait is accompanied by numerous conditions.

18 February President Gorbachev of the USSR presents a six-point peace plan.

19 February President Bush indicates that the Soviet plan 'is much less than what is necessary'.

22 February Baghdad communicates its acceptance of the Gorbachev plan. President Bush confirms that the Iraqi withdrawal from Kuwait must begin before 17.00 GMT on 23 February and must be completed within a week.

23 February Iraq allows the second Allied ultimatum to expire.

24 February Land operations begin before dawn: American, French and British troops enter Kuwait and Iraq.

25 February The Allies encounter very little resistance, and an impressive number of Iraqi soldiers give themselves up to Coalition soldiers almost as if they were a liberating army.

26 February Twenty-one Iraqi divisions have been destroyed; 40,000 of Baghdad's soldiers have been taken prisoner. The Republican Guard is incapable of halting the Allied advance.

27 February Kuwait city is liberated. In a tank battle between Iraqi and American tanks to the south of Basra, the Iraqis succumb once again. The Iraqi Ambassador to the United Nations announces the acceptance of all resolutions concerning Iraq. President George Bush announces to the USA and to the world that hostilities will cease as from 6.00 a.m. on 28 February.

DESERT STORM
THE GULF WAR IN COLOUR

It has been estimated that four million Iraqi men and women have volunteered to serve in the people's army. Aroused by years of propaganda, many of them have openly declared that they are willing to shed their blood for Saddam Hussein. (Canada Wide/Sygma/Grazia Neri)

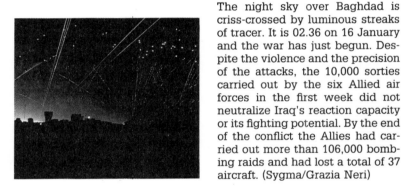

The night sky over Baghdad is criss-crossed by luminous streaks of tracer. It is 02.36 on 16 January and the war has just begun. Despite the violence and the precision of the attacks, the 10,000 sorties carried out by the six Allied air forces in the first week did not neutralize Iraq's reaction capacity or its fighting potential. By the end of the conflict the Allies had carried out more than 106,000 bombing raids and had lost a total of 37 aircraft. (Sygma/Grazia Neri)

From the first days of the war, Saddam Hussein tried to involve the whole of the Islamic world in his battle against the coalition and Israel. Although he put faith in the religious fanaticism and repressed hatred of the West, he did not succeed in his attempt. The governments of the principal Arab countries sided with the Allies, and even the terrorist actions repeatedly invoked by Saddam had extremely limited effect. (P. Robert/Sygma/Grazia Neri)

A launch pad for Hawk surface to air missiles stands out against the sunset in the Saudi Arabia desert. The probability of a surprise air or missile attack increases after nightfall and the night hours pass in constant fear of a new alarm. Hawk missiles are particularly effective against attacks launched at low and medium altitude, and they were widely deployed in Saudi Arabia to defend airports and Allied bases. (J. Ficara-Woodfin Camp/Grazia Neri)

From the first night, 16 January, the massive deployment of the radar-invisible F-117 Stealth fighter-bomber was of particular importance. This aircraft is capable of carrying out very precise attacks against the most highly protected command and control centres. Thanks to its particular geometry and the materials of which it is built, it is very difficult to spot this Black Jet on radar screens, and this means that it is not very vulnerable to attack even though its speed is limited. (Woodfin Camp/Grazia Neri)

The government-controlled Iraqi media never ceased to transmit propagandist images and news, but the initial enthusiasm soon gave way to desperation. Terrorized by the incessant hail of bombs, the population began to rebel and on 15 February the crowd killed ten leading members of the Baath party at Diwaniyed, 150 kilometres from Baghdad. (T. Kerni-Contact Press Images/Grazia Neri)

Bodies line the streets and on the means of public transport of Iraq cities. At 04.00 on 13 February, two Smart bombs, dropped by American bombers, penetrated a bunker in the Amriya quarter of Baghdad, killing more than 500 people. The Pentagon explained that the air-raid shelter was used as a command centre and claimed that the responsibility for these deaths was the premeditated madness of Saddam Hussein. (J. M. Bourget/Grazia Neri)

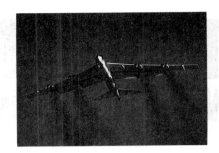

'Big, bad and ugly' is the term used by B-52 pilots to describe this enormous aircraft, which is the heaviest strategic bomber used by the USAF. These 'Stratofortresses' were deployed, despite their age, because they have a very complete defence avionics (even superior to that of the B1-B) and a greater load capacity. The B-52G has a combat speed of between 671 and 1018km/h and a ceiling of almost 15,000 metres. (G. Hall/Woodfin Camp/Grazia Neri)

In the first thirty days of the war the bombardments caused more than 20,000 Iraqi dead and 60,000 injured according to Baghdad, but the real figures are probably greater. The White House maintains that the majority of civilian victims were caused by the fact that Saddam Hussein had placed military installations in residential areas, near mosques and even inside schools. (J. M. Bourget/Paris Match/Grazia Neri)

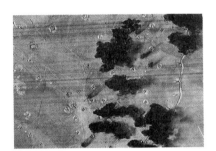

The effects of an American bombardment of Iraqi entrenched positions are clearly visible in this aerial photograph, taken by the crew of a B-52. In a conventional bombing mode, the Stratofortress is capable of transporting in its internal hold up to eighty-four 227kg bombs or 27 'cluster' bombs each weighting 454 kilograms. (Orban/Sygma/Grazia Neri)

The pilot of an F-15E flies over Kuwaiti territory during a daytime bombing mission. The Strike-Eagle is the most recent version of the F-15D and specializes in ground attacks. Thanks to its nocturnal tracking and navigation system, it can be deployed at any time. The picture clearly shows the ejector seat system and part of the cockpit. (G. Hall/Grazia Neri)

The pilot of a General Dynamics F-16 Fighting Falcon checks the position of his fellow formation member. In cases like these the pilots use a special terminology; the cockpit is ideally divided into sectors for an easier and speedier localization of the other aircraft. Looking ahead is known as '12 o'clock', right is '3 o'clock', towards the tail is '6 o'clock' and left is '9 o'clock'. Generally the fighters operate in pairs for mutual protection. (G. Hall/Woodfin Camp/Grazia Neri)

A dense cloud of smoke rises from a Kuwaiti oil refinery blown up by the Iraqi occupying army. Oil wells and oil processing installations were fired in an attempt to cause a collapse of the country's economy and hinder the bombing operations of the Allied air forces. At the end of the conflict 950 Kuwaiti oil wells had been destroyed or seriously damaged. (P. Durand/Sygma/Grazia Neri)

A General Dynamics F-16C photographed in solo flight in Saudi airspace. Sixty-eight of these aircraft were deployed in the theatre of operations. The Falcon is rightly considered one of the best offensive and defensive aircraft present in the Middle East. Well-armed and agile, the F-16 has a turbofan jet engine, produced by General Electric, which can develop a thrust of 12,520kg, enabling it to fly at speeds greater than Mach 2. (G. Hall/Woodfin Camp/Grazia Neri)

Never before had so much faith been placed in electronics as in the Gulf War. The picture shows some of the equipment of a B-52 bomber in which we can see the FLIR (Forward Looking Infrared) night vision system. This piece of equipment provides a black-and-white television image of what is immediately above and below the aircraft. (G. Hall/Woodfin Camp/Grazia Neri)

This F-15C is launching a Sparrow air-to-air missile. Many of these aircraft were equipped with AN/ALQ 131 equipment, which is a system of electronic countermeasures for self-defence and jamming. The Eagle is armed with an M61 cannon with six rotating 20mm barrels, which is extremely efficient at close-range. (Pool/Sygma/Grazia Neri)

It is the night of 17 January: an F-117 Stealth bomber carries out a precision attack on a multi-functional communications centre in the middle of Baghdad. A few moments later the building will be completely destroyed. The picture was taken by the bomber pilot using the particular infrared vision system with which the black jet is equipped. (Sygma/Grazia Neri)

The best-trained crews of the Italian Air Force were chosen to fly Italy's ten Tornadoes and they were almost all commandants or instructors from the 154th, 155th and 156th Flight Group. The Allied command and the pilots of the coalition air forces praised the Italian pilots who carried out the missions entrusted to them with great professionalism. (Italian Air Force)

Two American F-15C fighters on a reconnaissance mission. Already on the night of 16 January, these interceptors guaranteed the aerial superiority of the Allied forces, operating successfully in extremely difficult combat conditions. The USAF deployed a total of 48 such aircraft from the 1st, 33rd and 36th Squadrons of the Tactical Fighter Wing. (H. J. Kokola/Grazia Neri)

The technicians of the Italian Air Force played a decisive role in the success of Operation 'Locust' because they were able to maintain the electronic, avionic and weapons systems of Italy's ten Tornadoes at the Al Dhafra airbase in a perfect state of efficiency. The complete Italian contingent involved in operations in the Gulf consisted of more than 600 pilots and airmen. (Italian Air Force)

The Italian Tornadoes were based far behind the front line and about 1,100 kilometres from their targets. i.e., close to their maximum operating range. This meant that they had to be refuelled in flight in every mission they undertook. This type of manoeuvre was necessary so as not to be penalized by the amount of armament that could be transported. Along their flight paths, the crews rendezvoused with British and American tanker aircraft. (Italian Air Force)

On Sunday, 20 January, four days after the start of the conflict, the world looked on helplessly at the first real 'live' representation of the horrors of war. On that day Iraqi television transmitted the shocking images of the Allied pilots who had been shot down by Saddam's anti-aircraft defences. This is a photograph of 28-year-old Jeffrey Zaun, a lieutenant in the US Navy. (T. Muscionico/Contact Press Images/Grazia Neri)

In-flight refuelling of an Italian Tornado by a US Air Force KC-135 flying tanker. One of the most spectacular aspects of the logistic undertakings of the multinational force was the massive use of such tankers. About 50 of them were in service, and they helped to multiply Allied air power in the Gulf. The K-135 is capable of transporting 60,000 litres of kerosene 2,000 kilometres from its base. (Italian Air Force)

Captain Maurizio Cocciolone, aged 30, from the Abruzzo region in Italy, was the navigator of an Italian Tornado shot down on 18 January. This is the picture of him broadcast by Iraqi TV three days later. He was finally freed on 4 March after 45 days of captivity. There was no certain news of Major Bellini, the Tornado pilot, until he too was freed on 5 March. (T. Muscionico/Contact Press Images/Grazia Neri)

On 17 January the Italian parliament authorized the Italian contingent to enter into action. The operation was known as Operation 'Locust' and was commanded by Colonel Redditi. That same night, a Tornado with Major Bellini and Captain Cocciolone on board was shot down by Iraqi anti-aircraft defences. The two pilots were taken prisoner and were liberated at the beginning of March. In the meantime the Italian Air Force had successfully carried out 250 sorties. (Italian Air Force)

From August onwards, the TV announcer Migdad Murad became practically the only official Iraqi news source and, automatically, one of the most celebrated international video stars just behind CNN's Peter Arnett. Always impeccably dressed, with a handkerchief in his breast pocket, Murad took part in the second interrogation of the Allied pilots who had been shot down by Iraqi anti-aircraft defences. (J. Pavlovsky/Sygma/Grazia Neri)

Eyes staring blankly into space, face swollen and uniform in disarray, the pictures of the Allied prisoners in Iraqi hands were seen all over the world and upset public opinion with their dramatic crudity. The name of this pilot of the free Kuwaiti air force is still unknown, but the Allied command in Saudi Arabia received thousands of letters for him from well-wishers. (T, Muscionico/Contact Press Images/Grazia Neri)

A Scud missile has just fallen in Riyadh, and the first emergency workers are already on the scene. These missiles weigh more than a ton and are more than twelve metres long. They are the product of a rather imprecise technology, but this does not mean they are not to be feared. For the inhabitants of Israel, Saudi Arabia and Bahrain who saw 72 falling in the weeks of the war (more than 70 per cent of which were intercepted by Patriot missiles), these rockets of Saddam Hussein's represented the symbol of terror. (A. Suau/Black Star/Grazia Neri)

The most terrible image of the treatment meted out to the Allied prisoners who were subjected to continuous psychological and evident physical violence was this picture of the British pilot, Captain John Peters, aged 29. Head down and eyes closed, he was not even capable of pronouncing his own name. The pilots and other Allied military personnel were not released until after the ceasefire of 28 February. (T. Muscionico/Contact Press Images/Grazia Neri)

The Fairchild A-10A Thunderbolt II was successfully employed in its specific role against Iraqi armoured divisions thanks to its deadly GAU-BA Avenger cannon. This 30mm cannon with seven rotating barrels fires projectiles capable of piercing the armour of medium and heavy tanks. The firing rate is impressive and ranges from 2,100 to 4,200 shots per minute. The A-10s are heavy and ungainly, but they can take a lot of punishment. (G. Morris/Imapress/Grazia Neri)

During the night of 18 January the first Scud missiles fell on Israel, but without causing loss of life. Saddam Hussein sought to provoke Israel into involvement in the war, thus damaging the coalition. But the Israelis stayed out of the conflict. (Sygma/Grazia Neri)

A French pilot looking extremely pleased about the outcome of a mission. The principal combat efforts of the French Air Force was carried out by the Jaguars of the 11th Fighter Squadron of Toul, which deployed some of its aircraft in Saudi Arabia whence they took off to strike targets in Iraq and in Kuwait. Of joint French and British production, the Jaguar can transport an enormous load of weapons although its range of action decreases as the weapon load increases. (Gauthier/Imapress-Grazia Neri)

Two deaths caused by the explosions, another twenty the result of heart attacks, 304 wounded and suffocations caused by gas-masks was the final balance of the 39 Scud missiles that fell on Israel before the American ultimatum of 22 February. To this must be added the 200 homes destroyed and the 7,300 damaged. However, it is obviously not possible to calculate the serious inconveniences inflicted by Saddam Hussein on a people not formally involved in the war. (R. Castelnuovo/Contact Press Images/Grazia Neri)

After 46 years, Italian fighter aircraft were once more involved in combat. From 25 September onwards, ten Tornado fighter-bombers were deployed at the Al Dhafra air-base in Abu Dhabi to take part in the combat operations for the liberation of Kuwait. During the conflict between 16 and 20 flight crews and more than 300 specialists were present. In this photograph the crew of a Tornado discuss the flight with a technician. (Italian Air Force)

This shows with harsh realism the tragedy experienced by Israel during the terrible days of the Gulf conflict. None the less the vast majority of Israelis approved their government's decision not to react to missile attacks so as not to play the Iraqi dictator's game. At the end of the conflict it was said that, for the first time in forty years, Israel had won a war without having to fight. (Sygma/Grazia Neri)

Jaguar strike aircraft taxi along the runway of a Saudi airfield before taking off on a bombing mission. The result of British and French collaboration, the Sepecat Jaguar has a working range of 1,408 kilometres. The two Turboméca Adour Rolls-Royce engines provide a thrust of 2,425kg enabling the aircraft to reach a maximum speed at sea level of 1,305km/h. During the war in the Gulf, Great Britain deployed twelve of these aircraft and France deployed 20. (J. Langevin/Sygma/Grazia Neri)

The pilots of a French squadron examine the map of a sector of occupied Kuwait shortly before setting off on a bombing mission. As well as twenty Jaguars, France also deployed ten Mirage F1C jets, which were used for aerial defence and attack. (J. C. Sauer/Paris Match/Grazia Neri)

During take-off and landing the wingspan of the Tornado opens to its maximum. Italian, British and Saudi Tornadoes carried out many missions of great strategic importance and made their contribution to ensuring Allied air supremacy. (Italian Air Force)

Protected by special overalls to protect them against chemical attack, these French technicians are positioning the armament of a Jaguar. The armament of this French Air Force aircraft weighs almost five tons and includes two DEFA 30mm cannon, free-fall bombs, Magic missiles and the deadly Martel anti-radar missile, which revealed itself to be extremely efficient in taking out Iraqi defensive systems. (Sygma/Grazia Neri)

Two F-15C fighter-interceptors of the Saudi Royal Air Force armed with Sidewinder missiles equipped with an infrared homing device for close combat. On 25 January, Captain Ayedh, piloting an Eagle, shot down two Iraqi Mirage F1 jets by launching missiles of this type. It should be remembered that, even today, nineteen years after its first appearance, the F-15 is still considered one of the West's most reliable and efficient interceptors. (J. Ficara/Woodfin Camp/Grazia Neri)

The aerial war has been in progress now for sixteen days and the confidence of this French pilot is a clear indicator of how greatly the Iraqi anti-aircraft defences have been weakened. The Jaguar is one of the first combat aircraft in the world to have wing racks on top of the wings for air-to-air missiles. This rather unusual formula was successfully experimented with in the course of the numerous missions carried out during the conflict. (J. C. Sauer/Parls Match/Grazia Neri)

A British Sea Harrier photographed while taking off vertically. Although this version of this unique combat aircraft was not deployed in the Gulf, the US Marines did deploy the AV-8B version. As in the Falklands War of 1982, the Harrier proved itself to be a most potent combat aircraft. (D. Fracchia/Grazia Neri)

The pilot of this Apache helicopter wears special night-vision glasses (NVG), which provide him with a more immediately and instinctive peripheral vision than the FLIR system. These special binoculars contain amplification systems for environmental light, and the illumination of the dashboard must be compatible with them. (Impact Photos/Grazia Neri)

This photograph gives some idea of the extreme complexity of a modern combat aircraft. The pilot of a B-52 controls the flow of eight Pratt and Whitney turbojet engines, with 7,710kg of thrust. (G. Hall/Woodfin Camp/Grazia Neri)

Some British pilots photographed near a Tornado at an RAF base in Saudi Arabia. The British Government sent forty-two IDS (Interdictor Strike) Tornadoes for ground attacks and eighteen ADV (Air Defence Variant) Tornadoes to the Gulf area. The RAF airmen suffered heavy losses due principally to the fact that bombing raids were carried out at very low altitudes. One pilot commented, 'We looked the camels in the eye'. (Sygma/Grazia Neri)

A Jaguar of the French Air Force opens fire with its 68mm multiple rocket-launchers. This small, agile, well-armed and rather speedy aircraft played an important role in providing tactical support by attacking ground targets right from the start of the war. Despite the danger inherent in this type of action, no Jaguars were shot down. (Jennifer/Imapress/Grazia Neri)

Once again the mighty B-52 strategic bomber the 'Stratofortress' here launching a cruise missile, demonstrated their enhanced attack potential, transporting both conventional bombs and cruise missiles. Designed thirty-six years ago, and used extensively in Vietnam, the B-52 can drop 22,680kg of bombs and has an action range of 7,010 kilometres without in-flight refuelling. (Compix/ Antinea/Grazia Neri)

Two British Westland Sea King helicopters have just taken off from HMS *Argus*, their mother ship, for a reconnaissance mission. Derived from the American Sikorsky S-61, these helicopters can be used in anti-ship and anti-submarine operations as well as for mine-hunting and rescue missions. The machine-gunner, in the left defensive position, is brandishing an FN 7.62mm GPNG, which has a very high rate of fire. (Impact Photos/Grazia Neri)

An F-14 Tomcat interceptor has just launched a Phoenix AIM-54 missile. This powerful two-seater fighter with a variable wingspan is the main aircraft used by the US Navy for the air defence of its naval units. With a maximum take-off weight of 33,720kg the Tomcat is the world's heaviest fighter to operate from a ship. The aircraft in the photograph belongs to Squadron UF84 'Jolly Rogers', easily recognized by the skull and cross-bones chosen as their symbol. (Sygma/Grazia Neri)

The Grumman E-2C Hawkeye is the US Navy's eye in the sky. This peculiarly shaped aircraft is a flying command post capable of controlling the air-space around the fleet as well as coordinating operations and providing all necessary information for operational decisions. The disc visible on the back of the aircraft contains the rotating aerial of the radar equipment. (Todd Buchanan/ Philadelphia Inquirer Matrix/ Grazia Neri)

The *England* launching an Extended Range Standard surface-to-air missile. The Pentagon deployed about eighty ships in the Persian Gulf and the Red Sea, including eight aircraft carriers, two battleships, a helicopter ship and numerous lesser units. These were flanked by more than fifty other units sent by coalition members, an impressive concentration of firepower, which also made use of the latest generation of missiles. (Photri/Grazia Neri)

This Tomcat has just taken off from the deck of an aircraft carrier. Some navy squadrons have been equipped with the new F-14-Plus version which has more powerful F-110 engines. In the foreground, with folded wings, is an AG-E Intruder equipped with the RAM navigation system, which enables it to carry out nocturnal missions against specific targets using 'Paveway' guided bombs. (Sygma/ Grazia Neri)

A Tomahawk missile launched from a quadruple MK-143 armoured launching ramp installed on a *Spruance*-class destroyer. In the first stages of the conflict American naval units launched about 250 cruise missiles. Cruise BGM 109C missiles are precise and lethal, with a range of about 1,300 kilometres and are very difficult to intercept. They were used to attack particularly important targets such as Scud launching sites, and their margin of error was very low. (Sygma/Grazia Neri)

The US aircraft carrier *Saratoga* (CV-59), seen here in the Red Sea, is 317 metres long and has a crew of 5,390 men. Built in 1956, she is propelled by conventional engines and can reach a speed of 33 knots. The US Navy sent more than half of its fourteen aircraft carriers to the Middle East. These units were drawn from the 2nd, 6th and 7th Fleets. (Sygma/Grazia Neri)

The American battleship *Missouri* shells the coast of occupied Kuwait with her 16in guns. The guns of *Missouri* and *Wisconsin* are each capable of firing one-ton shells up to a distance of 40 kilometres. The Japanese surrender was signed aboard this ship, which was extensively re-equipped in the 1970s and 1980s. (Sygma/Grazia Neri)

An F-14 fighter photographed a few seconds before taking off from USS *Saratoga*. The Tomcat is the main high-performance interceptor used by the US Navy and is deployed on all the major aircraft carriers. Its performance is comparable to that of the F-15, and its task is to defend the fleet to which it is assigned. It is armed with a 20mm cannon and can carry a maximum of eight air-to-air missiles, including AIM-54C Phoenix long-range missiles. (T. Hartwell/ Grazia Neri)

Protected by a heavy asbestos suit and garish ear protectors, a technician on the aircraft carrier *Saratoga* enjoys a rare moment of relaxation while waiting for the bombers to come back. *Saratoga* is a conventionally propelled assault aircraft carrier with a displacement of 80,000 tons. It transports 75 aircraft including F-18 Hornet multi-purpose fighters and the old but still efficient A-7 Corsair II bombers, which are clearly visible, wings folded. (A. Keler/Sygma/Grazia Neri)

The naval component of the Italian forces present in the Gulf deployed about a thousand sailors and some soldiers from the Battaglione San Marco, who were responsible for security. On the morning of 3 January the guided missile destroyer *Audace* set off for the Persian Gulf to relieve the frigate *Orsa* from her patrol and observation missions. On 19 January she joined the escort of the aircraft carrier *Roosevelt*. (N. Leto/Epipress/Grazia Neri)

On 25 January, Saddam Hussein ordered two billion litres of oil to be dumped into the sea from the installations at Mina al Hamadi, causing an ecological disaster of terrifying proportions. An enormous oil slick floating on the surface of the waters of the Gulf destroys all forms of life while hundreds of cormorants, their feathers covered in oil, throw themselves onto the beach almost as if they were invoking death – innocent symbols of human folly. (P. Durand/Sygma/Grazia Neri)

The *Audace* also had the task of searching for floating mines in the Gulf. These old-fashioned explosive devices, similar to those used in the Second World War, only explode if hit, but they contain up to half a ton of TNT and can cause serious damage. At night the sea surface was kept under surveillance using a special night vision instrument that enables one to see in the dark. (N. Leto-Epipress/Grazia Neri)

Desperate and certain of defeat, the Iraqis set fire to Kuwait's oil wells one by one, perhaps in the hope that the curtain of smoke created by the combustion of the oil might help to cover their retreat. After a first estimate of damage, experts believe that it will take four years to put out all the fires and that the reconstruction of the wells will cost about 25 billion dollars. (Owen/Black Star/Grazia Neri)

During the day it was the helicopters that did most of the patrolling. The picture shows an Augusta-Bell 212 ASV stationed on *Audace* as it takes off on a mine-spotting mission. This helicopter is the result of collaboration between the US and Italian air forces and is particularly suited for such tasks because of the sophisticated sonar system with which it is equipped. The A-B 212 is also highly appreciated by its crews because of its exceptional robustness and reliability. (N. Leto/Epipress/Grazia Neri)

The dimensions of the black oil slick caused by the release of more than eleven million barrels of oil into the water of the Persian Gulf are frightening; 80 kilometres in length and 15 kilometres wide. The gravity of the ecological damage has been increased by the fact that, because of the war, it was impossible to intervene immediately. However, numerous countries have offered Saudi Arabia their complete economic and technological support. (P. Durand/Sygma/Grazia Neri)

According to Pentagon instruction, the women enrolled in the American armed forces cannot participate in combat operations. During Operation 'Desert Storm' they drove supply trucks, checked missile-launching systems and worked in field hospitals. In particular the women of the 101st Airborne Division piloted many of the 300 helicopters that transported 2,000 men and hundreds of weapons and means of transport into Iraqi territory. (J. C. Coutasse/Contact Press Images/Grazia Neri)

A dense blanket of smoke blackens the sky over Kuwait. The wells have now been burning for days and many more will pass before the flames are put out. The Texan company led by 'Red' Adair, who is considered the world's most expert oil-well firefighter, is ready to intervene as soon as the political situation has been stabilized. Only then will it be possible to evaluate the real extent of the damage. (D. Hudson/Sygma/Grazia Neri)

Saddam Hussein's armoured divisions could do very little against the Apache helicopters that soon became a nightmare for them. Indeed, many of them preferred to surrender without putting up a fight when faced with this anti-tank helicopter, which mounts a 30mm cannon and can fire up to 1,200 rounds per minute. It also has laser-guided Hellfire missiles, which are extremely precise. The tracking of all the weapons follows the movement of the pilot's helmet, and the crew is protected by armour plating that can withstand machine-gun fire. (A. Suau/Black Star/Grazia Neri)

Laden with heavy equipment, a Marine seeks refreshment with a few cans of beer. Especially in the months of August and September, the high temperatures in the Saudi Arabian desert caused a good few problems for the supply of water to the troops. On average, each soldier drank one litre of water per hour. The personal weapon issued to the Marines is now the A2 version of the M-16 rifle, but this Marine is equipped with an M-60 machine-gun. (D. Turnley/Black Star/Grazia Neri)

On board a light 4-wheel-drive Hummer vehicle, three American soldiers drive up close to the village of Khafji. Repulsed by the Allies after fierce fighting, Saddam's troops suffered heavy losses and retreated leaving behind about 400 prisoners in the hands of Saudi forces. One can see clearly in the photograph the dense cloud of smoke on the horizon, which was caused by the burning of an oil refinery that Saddam's troops blew up. (D. Hudson/Sygma/Grazia Neri)

90,000 Marines from training camps in Georgia and Virginia were sent to the Gulf as part of the American expedition force. After Vietnam, Grenada and Panama, once again the Marines were the first to reach the crisis zone with an air bridge from Fort Bragg just a few days after Iraqi troops invaded Kuwait on 2 August. (J. C. Coutasse/Contact Press Images/Grazia Neri)

General Norman Schwarzkopf, the commander of the American expedition in the Middle East, inspects troops on the day before the land offensive. Nicknamed the 'Bear' because of his irascibility and his massive build, he demonstrated an exceptional ability in coordination and military strategy, which were decisive factors in guaranteeing perfect harmony between the troops of 28 allied nations. (D. Turnley/Black Star/Grazia Neri)

On the night of 29 January, Iraqi armoured forces invaded the town of Khafji on the Saudi-Kuwaiti border. General Schwarzkopf defined the battle to regain control of the town 'a mosquito bite', but for the Allied soldiers it was the first terrible occasion on which they found themselves face to face with the enemy. In the photograph, a shocked Saudi soldier looks at the charred remains of an Iraqi soldier killed in the burned-out wreck of an armoured car. (G. Morris/Black Star/Grazia Neri)

An American artillery position is pounding the Iraqi trenches in Kuwait. During Operation 'Desert Storm' the United States could count on a force of 380,000 soldiers, including 27,000 women, who were equipped with more than 1,500 tanks. To this figure must be added the 70,000 men of the Marine Corps. Cover for these troops was provided by more than 300 Apache and Cobra combat helicopters. (G. Morris/Black Star/Grazia Neri)

After two days of fighting and incessant artillery fire, Allied forces managed to regain control of the village, which the Iraqis had invaded with tanks while pretending they wanted to give themselves up. The battle of Khafji was the first land battle of the conflict, and the Allied troops were able to find out just how bloody it was to fight against Iraqi troops who had been toughened by eight years of war with Iran. (G. Morris/Black Star/Grazia Neri)

A Marine, armed with an M16-A with a high precision sight, observes the front line, which is but a few kilometres distant. The Marines were the protagonists of the helicopter-transported assault in Iraqi territory and later of the conquest of the strategic island of Faylaka and the battle for the liberation of Kuwait City Airport. They were led by General Walter Boomer, one of six key men in the American contingent. (D. Hudson/Sygma/Grazia Neri)

At the end of the battle, the Iraqis left 200 dead and 80 tanks and armoured vehicles on the battlefield, most of which had been destroyed by A-10 Thunderbolt aircraft and by Allied warships, whose fire was guided via radio by Marines trapped in the city. The Americans lost eleven Marines at Khafji, while two, including the woman soldier, Melissa Rathburn, were captured. The young American woman was released on 4 March, after the ceasefire. (G. Morris/Black Star/Grazia Neri)

The sky over the Saudi Arabian Desert is illuminated by the wakes of rockets launched by 227mm MLRS launchers. These were used during the Battle of Khafji and to open up a breach for the Allied armoured troops during the offensive that began on 24 February. They are capable of hitting targets far beyond the range of conventional artillery and form part of the equipment used by American, British and Saudi divisions. (Orban/Sygma/Grazia Neri)

The men of the 82nd Airborne Division who took up position on the border between Saudi Arabia and Kuwait on 8 August were equipped with highly sophisticated means to defend themselves against chemical weapons. These two soldiers, photographed during manoeuvres, are wearing gasmasks and using smoke-bombs, which would provide cover for their movement during an assault. (Sygma/Grazia Neri)

From the start it was clear that there was a minimal resistance to the crack French assault troops and on the evening of 24 February soldiers of the Foreign Legion were able to prepare large areas as landing pads for Puma and Gazelle combat helicopters, which are armed with anti-tank missiles. An efficient radio link was quickly established to allow communication in real time between the Allied command and the advanced outposts in Iraqi territory. (J. C. Coutasse/Contact Press Images/ Grazia Neri)

Fear of the possible use of chemical weapons by the Iraqi army was one of the principal issues in the Gulf war. According to CIA experts, the land and air-transported Iraqi troops had large quantities of poisonous material ready for use. It should be remembered that, during the war with Iran, Saddam Hussein had ordered bombardments of chemical weapons, including some against the population of Kurdistan. (Orban/Sygma/ Grazia Neri)

When the ultimatum given to Saddam Hussein expired on 24 February the coalition forces launched their attack. The first to move were the men of the French Foreign Legion, who, with hundreds of tanks, and armoured vehicles and with the protection of their artillery, began to advance towards Iraqi outposts in the north-east of the Arabian peninsula, not far from the city of Hafar Al Batin on the border between Iraq and Kuwait. (Sygma/Grazia Neri)

Only at the end of the conflict was it discovered that the use of chemical weapons had been hindered by the precision bombing raids, which destroyed the majority of Iraqi stores as well as the complex logistics and communications system needed for the efficient use of such systems. As well as his normal equipment, this Marine has in his rucksack all the equipment necessary to defend and protect himself in case of chemical attack. (D. Turnley/ Black Star/Grazia Neri)

The French government sent three regiments of the Foreign Legion to the Gulf; 3,000 well trained, professionals with experience of war in the desert. The land contingent, led by General Michel Roguejoffre, formerly commander of the French rapid intervention force (FAR), consisted of about 12,000 men, 120 helicopters, 40 AMX 30 B-2 tanks and twenty-four mechanically towed 155mm artillery pieces. (J. C. Coutasse/Contact Press Images/Grazia Neri)

A column of Allied tanks advances across the sands of the Kuwaiti desert. It is 25 February and, with slightly more than 24 hours gone since the start of the land offensive, more than 20,000 Iraqi soldiers have surrendered. During the conflict the coalition forces deployed more than 4,600 armoured vehicles, including French AMX-30 MBTs, British Chieftain Mk 5 and Challenger MBTs and the American-made Abrams. (Sygma/Grazia Neri)

Endless lines of Legionnaires advance in the desert in prohibitive climatic conditions. Some of them carry launching systems for MILAN wire-guided missiles. This weapon is particularly precise because, once the operator has taken aim and the target is in his sights, he can direct the missile directly to the target by means of a wire that is unrolled from the fins of the missile. (J. C. Coutasse/ Contact Press Images/Grazia Neri)

An Apache helicopter on a patrol and attack mission during the advance into Iraq territory, which was planned so as to encircle the Republican Guard. At dawn on 24 February, 2,000 men of the airborne assault troops launched the most imposing aerial cavalry operation in history. In a few hours, 118 helicopters, some of them piloted by women, penetrated hundreds of miles into enemy territory transporting tons of weapons and supplies. (T. Stoddart/Katz/Grazia Neri)

A French marksman with the barrel of his precision rifle wrapped in cloth to protect it from the devastating effects of heat and sand. At times the temperature rose to more than 50°C, and it appears that there were cases when the temperatures reached such a level that they caused deformation of the barrels of armoured vehicles without protective covering on them. (J. C. Coutasse/Contact Press Images/ Grazia Neri)

Lying in wait among the dunes, the Legionnaires wait for a possible sortie by Iraqi tanks. They have just disembarked from a Puma transport helicopter, and the men of this brigade have already taken up their positions. The man in the front line is armed with a light anti-tank weapon, the explosive charge of which is capable of piercing the defensive plating of a heavy armoured vehicle. (J. C. Coutasse/Contact Press Images/ Grazia Neri)

The expression these Iraqi prisoners have on their tired and care-worn faces is not fear or even resignation. What one can read is the relief of having put an end to days of anguish, fear and difficulties by their surrender. They arrive from all parts of the desert escorted by a few Allied soldiers and patiently wait to be sent to collection camps. There were already about 20,000 prisoners a day and a half after the start of the attack. (J. Langevin/Sygma/Grazia Neri)

A few hours after the expiry of the ultimatum of 23 February the British 'Desert Rats' also began their assault deep into Iraqi territory. Just a few days previously, during manoeuvres, these men had jokingly talked about their conviction and desire to reach Baghdad. (D. Hudson/Sygma/ Grazia Neri)

An Iraqi soldier shows one of the thousand of leaflets illustrating how to surrender that were dropped behind enemy lines by Allied aircraft right from the first days of the war. As well as having the purely practical task of facilitating communication between men of different tongues, they were also designed negatively to influence the psychology of the Iraqis and induce them to abandon their weapons. (J. Langevin/Sygma/ Grazia Neri)

The soldiers of the 1st British Armoured Division, known as the 'Desert Rats' were among those spearheading the Allied offensive. they went into action beyond the Saudi Arabian border and had the task of facing up to Saddam Hussein's Republic Guard. The British government sent about 36,000 men into the Gulf. They were all professionals and, with the Americans, formed the strontest contingent of coalition forces. (D. Hudson/Sygma/ Grazia Neri)

While Radio Baghdad was announcing in triumphal tones the killing of 10,000 American soldiers and the destruction of the aircraft carrier, Saratoga, exhausted Iraqi forces were surrendering to coalition troops. The Saddam line collapsed and crumbled when faced with the overpowering strategic and technological superiority of the Allies in the same way as the ideological fanaticism, which had nurtured an entire people for months, was extinguished by suffering and fear. (Orban/Sygma/ Grazia Neri)

The land troops sent by Great Britain consisted of 29,000 men, of whom 20,000 were deployed in the front line. The weaponry and *matériel* at their disposal were impressive: 160 Challenger tanks, 300 Warrior and Scorpion armoured vehicles and hundreds of other vehicles of various types. The artillery comprised of sixty-four 155mm guns and a battery of twelve multiple rocket-launchers as well as 80 combat helicopters. (D. Hudson/Sygma/Grazia Neri)

'You have fought with courage, now retreat.' It was with these words that Radio Baghdad announced the end of hostilties. For thousands of Iraqi soldiers that war had already come to an end. 'There is no aversion towards the enemy, rather the hatred is reserved for Saddam Hussein who wanted a useless massacre, a war fought in the name of his delirious thirst for power'. (Orban/Sygma/ Grazia Neri)

The British 'Desert Rats', whose namesakes, the 7th Armoured Division, led by General Montgomery, defeated Rommel's Afrika Korps in the North African Desert. Their equipment comprises a total of 75 accessories with a total weight of about 25 kilograms. The British contingent was commanded by General Peter de la Billière, who was appointed by Margaret Thatcher shortly before her resignation. (D. Hudson/Sygma/Grazia Neri)

The large number of prisoners, which exceeded all expectations, also created serious logistic problems. Everything turned out to be inadequate; the means of transport, the camps set up in the desert, medical assistance and supplies. Allied forces regard with dismay their defeated enemies, and the only emotions they experience are of pity and compassion. (D. Hudson/Sygma/Grazia Neri)

A group of Iraqi prisoners being captured by Marines on Kuwaiti soil. In the background can be seen some of the 950 oil wells which Saddam Hussein's troops blew up as a reprisal. The ecological disaster brought about by these vandalistic actions is of extraordinary dimensions as is the economic damage. (G. Morris/Black Star/Grazia Neri)

These are the last dramatic sequences of the battle to reconquer Kuwait City by coalition troops. An Iraqi soldier is captured and frisked by American soldiers on the outskirts of the capital along the A5 motorway. These moments of high tension were followed by a period of great elation and joy. (P. Durand/Sygma/Grazia Neri)

An Iraqi combat tank in flames after being hit by a TOW air-to-ground missile launched from an Apache helicopter. The Iraqi army had 4,200 tanks before the start of the war, but the devastating combat actions of the coalition troops destroyed 3,700 of them. (G. Morris/Black Star/Grazia Neri)

On the morning of 27 February, during the bloodiest phases of the battle to liberate Kuwait City, men from the Special Forces are trying to draw out the last Iraqi soldiers, who are principally concentrated around the American Embassy. In their hurried flight, the soldiers of the defeated army abandoned hundreds of booty-laden vehicles along the roads leading north because they had run out of petrol. (D. Hudson/Sygma/Grazia Neri)

The crew of an LVTP-7A1 amphibious armoured personnel carrier (APT) of the US Marines observes from a distance a Kuwaiti oil well set on fire by Iraqi soldiers before their retreat. This armoured vehicle is protected by active defence plates, which, thanks to their explosive charges, guarantee an effective defence against hollow charge armour piercing shells. (G. Morris/Black Star/Grazia Neri)

Marines frisking a man suspected of being an Iraqi officer, who is attempting to flee with his family. Although he is dressed in civilian clothes, he was carrying a Soviet-made pistol like those generally used by Iraqi non-commissioned officers. In their hurried flight north, many Iraqi soldiers sought to escape with loot, particularly electrical goods, but were almost immediately forced to abandon their bulky items of booty. (D. Hudson/Sygma/Grazia Neri)

After Saddam Hussein's announcement of the withdrawal from Kuwait on 26 February, Iraqi soldiers desperately sought to escape on any available vehicle. The fleeing soldiers were overcome by terror and panic and the retreat quickly turned into a disorganized rout which enabled the Allied helicopters and armoured cars to inflict serious losses on the enemy. (J. Langevin/Sygma/Grazia Neri)

Finally liberated, the inhabitants of Kuwait City come out to greet coalition troops, holding out hands in sign of brotherhood and gratitude. Women cry and smiling children try to climb up onto the armoured cars. Just outside the city, in the desert, the war goes on and the sombre thunder of explosions could be heard over the crowd's shouts of joy. (P. Durand/Sygma/Grazia Neri)

The flight north was tragic for the Iraqi troops. Exhausted by weeks of continuous bombardments, by difficulties with communications and provisions and depressed by the progress of the war, they presented easy targets for the Allies. The road towards Basra appeared to be completely blocked by vehicles of all types, buses, tracked vehicles, cars and jeeps easily destroyed by the air forces of the Allied powers, lie abandoned, a tragic symbol of the rout. (D. Hudson/Sygma/Grazia Neri)

At the end of the battle the American troops stood aside to allow the troops of the Emirate to enter the city first. After seven months of terror, the population was able to embrace its own soldiers, walk along the city streets and rejoice at the end of a nightmare. (J. Langevin/Sygma/Grazia Neri)

All traces of the Iraqi occupation were immediately and systematically destroyed. Portraits of Saddam Hussein were obliterated, and murals with the image of the dictator were broken into little pieces with hammers and picks. The inhabitants of Kuwait city want to eliminate all traces of this tragic period, to rebuild their country and return to live in a climate of peace and liberty. (Durand-Langevin/Sygma/Grazia Neri)

Overcome by uncontrollable joy, these women greet the liberation of the country by raising the portrait of Sheikh Jaber Al Sabah, who succeeded his cousin Salem to the throne in 1978. A capable administrator of the nation's wealth, it was he who organized the shrewd policy of reinvesting his country's petrol revenue in international financial markets, and this policy made the small Kuwait a world-class financial power. (Durand-Langevin/Sygma/ Grazia Neri)

An apocalyptic scene provides the backdrop to the victory of the Allied forces in the Kuwaiti capital – the smoke of hundreds of burning oil wells comes between the troops who enter the city in triumph. The spectral light seems to enhance the drama of the defeated Iraqis who are fleeing in a northerly direction. (J. Langevin/ Sygma/Grazia Neri)

Kuwait city was isolated from the rest of the world for seven months, and there was no possibility of communication that was not controlled by the Iraqi occupiers. It is not yet clear exactly what happened during this period, but there is talk of deaths, torture and terrible cruelty. After the joy, sorrow will return with the memory of the victims and the dismay for the devastation. What is important now is that today the Emir's flag is flying once more over Kuwait city. (J. Langevin/ Sygma/Grazia Neri)

Kuwait city is free, peace has returned to the land and it is time for celebration. When the euphoria has passed it will be time to rebuild a devastated nation. Al-Shehean, the Emir's right-hand man, was given the job of organizing a massive reconstruction plan, which involves th re-activation of the oil wells, the repair of bridges and roads as well as the reconstruction of damaged buildings – an enormous task with an estimated cost of more than fifty billion pounds. (J. Langevin/ Sygma/Grazia Neri)

President Bush is welcomed enthusiastically by American soldiers on the occasion of his visit to the Gulf on 20 November. This picture became the symbol of the bond between the President and his 'boys'. America had never previously shown as much cohesion as during this period, and the patriotic spirit has never been so strong. Bush's popularity reached the stars, and according to some polls nine out of ten Americans fully support the actions of the President. (J. L. Atlan/Sygma/ Grazia Neri)

Norman Schwarzkopf, US Army General and commander of the Allied troops in the Gulf, finally serene after the liberation of Kuwait city and the great success of land operations, congratulates his victorious troops. He has a close relationship with them, and he planned and carried out the crushing victory over the Iraqi army while trying to limit losses among his own troops as much as possible. (D. Turnley/Grazia Neri)

Acknowledgements
The publishers wish to acknowledge the assistance of
Grazia Neri, Marco Finazzi, Anna Galliani, Luciano
Alberti and Gianna Manferto in the production of this
book; with special thanks to Stato Maggiore dell'
Aeronautica Militare Italiana. The photographs were
taken by photographers from the Grazia Neri Agency
except for those depicting Italian aircraft and pilots,
which were kindly supplied by the Italian Air Force.

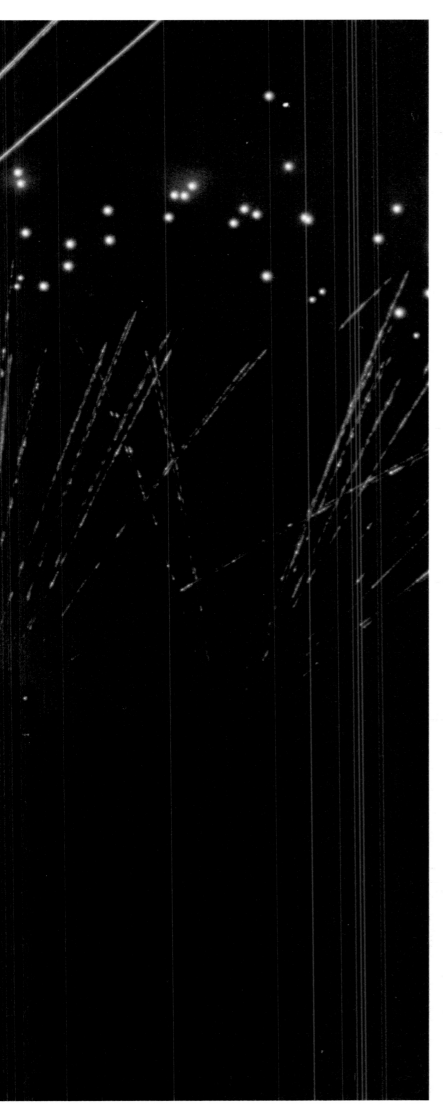

المهيب الركن صدام حسين رئيس الجمهورية والقائد العام للقوات المسلحة

دار الحرية للطباعة

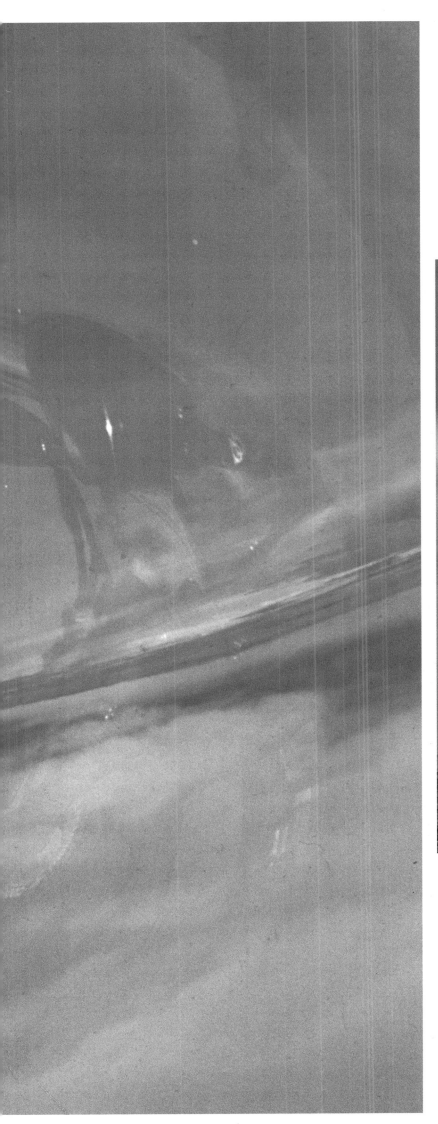

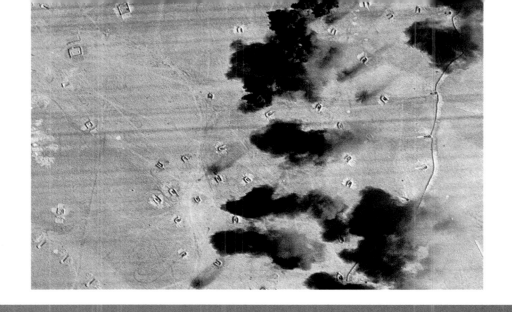

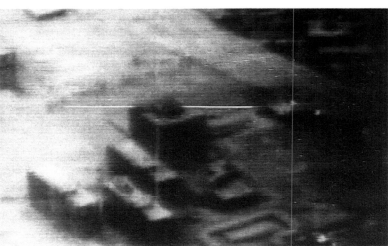

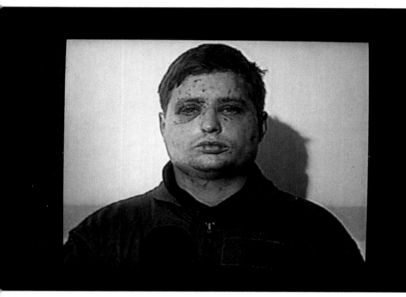

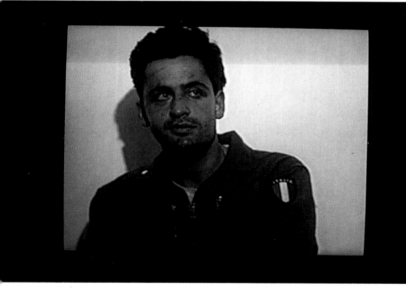

ITHFUL SERVANT
OF GOD
ODAM HUSSEIN

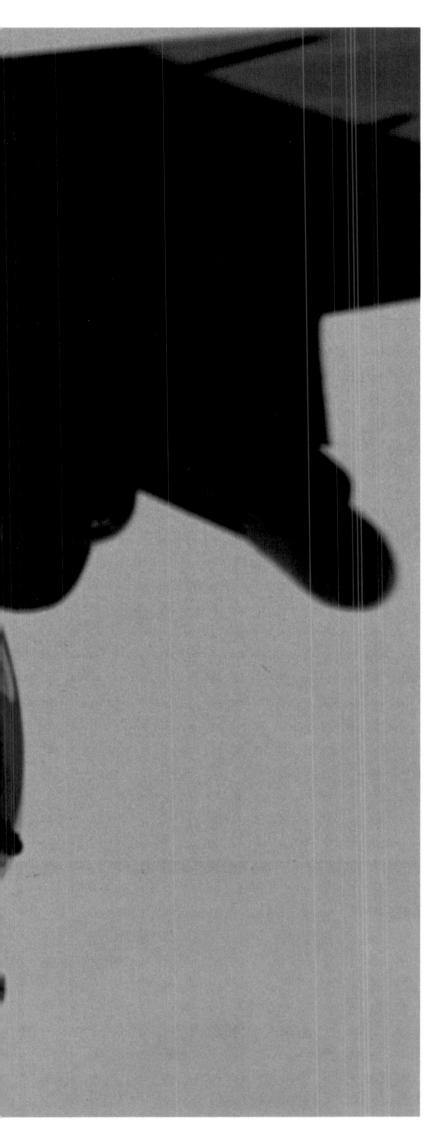

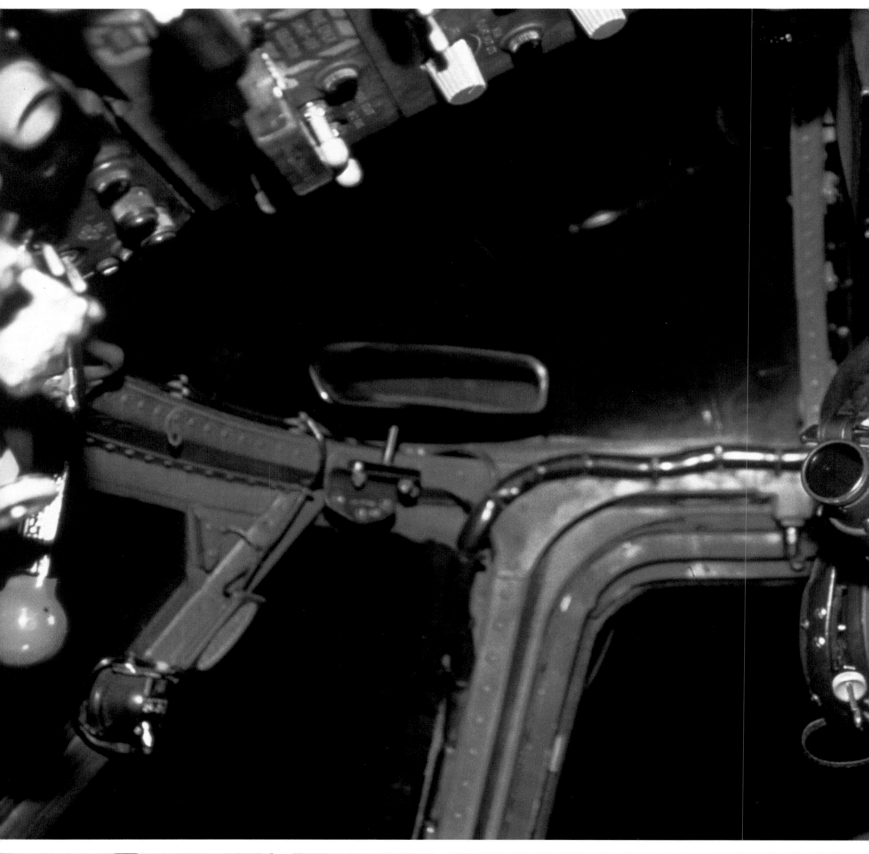

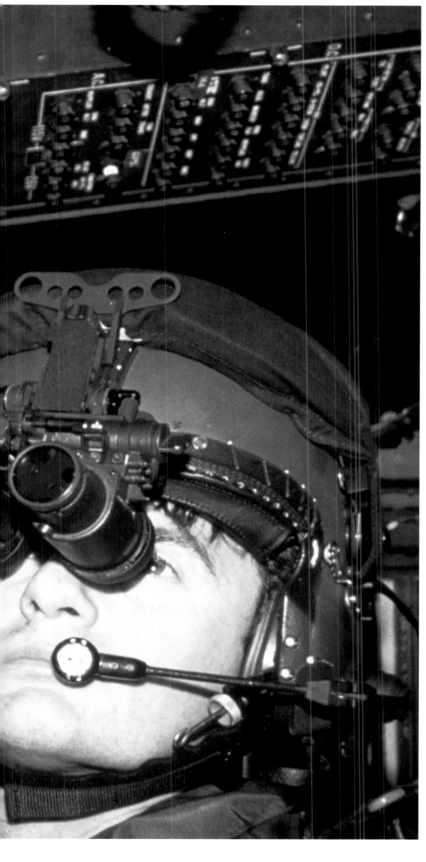

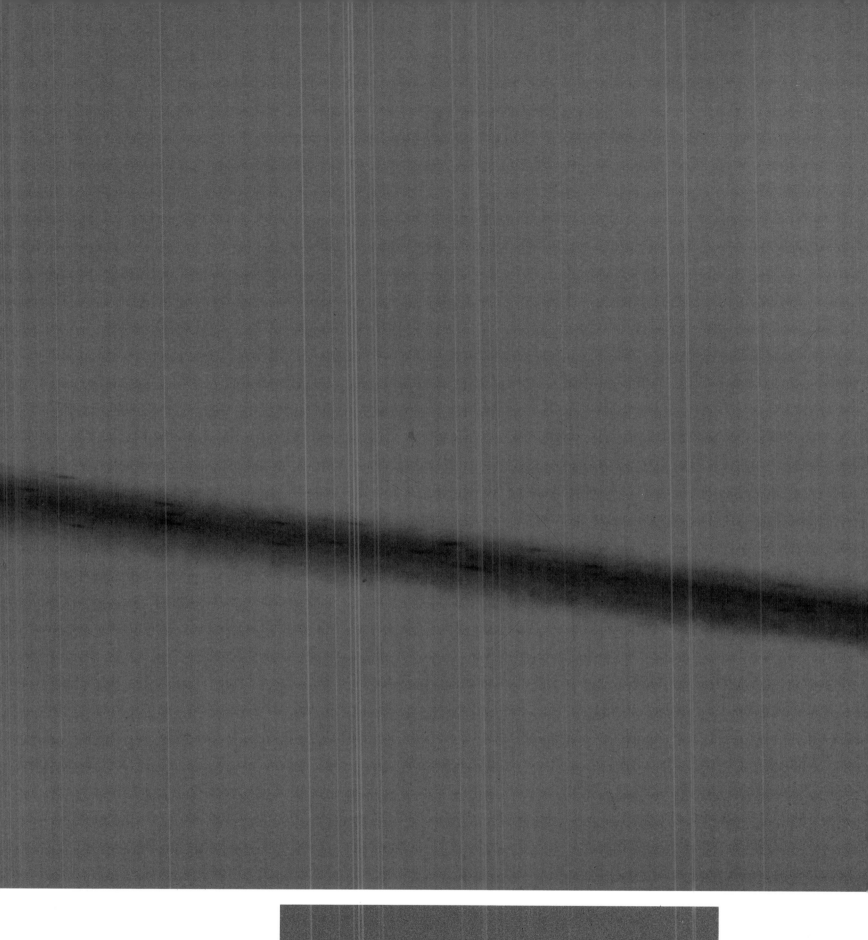

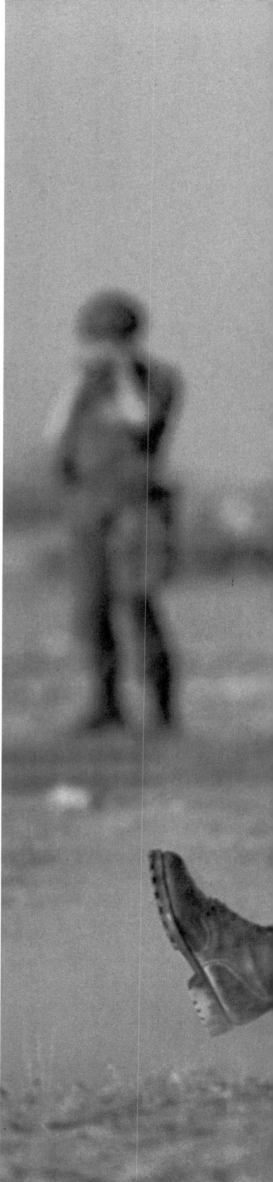

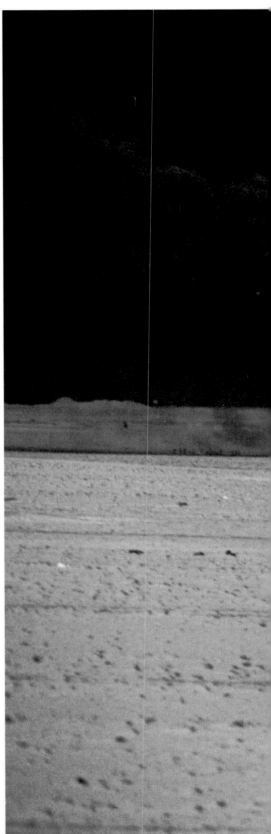